EARN YOUR BREAD ONLINE

ART OF MAKING MONEY ONLINE

BHAVIK DHANVANI

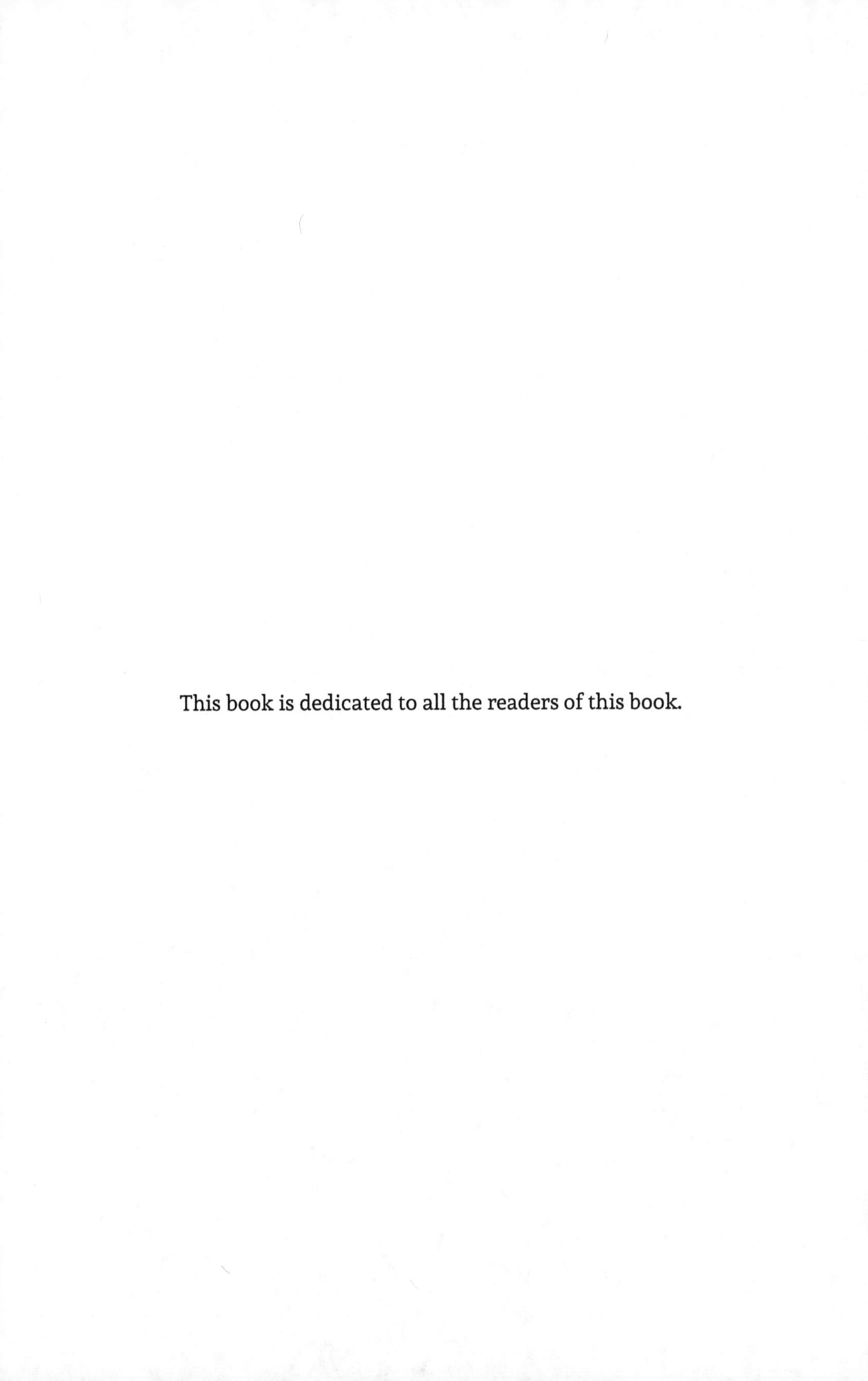

This book is dedicated to all the readers of this book.

Contents

Foreword

As we know everyone nowadays is looking to make money from their comfort zone i.e from home or any place in the world. In this eBook you will get all the possible ways to make money online. You just need a Laptop or computer and a stable Internet connection that's it, so no one can stop you to make money online. All possible ways are tested by the experts and everyone is making money online.

Once you read this Book I am sure you will make money online within a couple of days and you can earn thousands of dollars per month. This Book is really helpful for the people who are looking to make money online and also it is helpful for the beginners.

Take Away- You can start in genuine way from today and see the difference. You don't have to work 9 to 5 for these ways, you can work anytime and anywhere. What are you waiting for? Just start making money today.

Acknowledgements

Initially, writing a book was tough task for me but on the other side it seemed more interesting because you can present your thoughts in front of audience. Hence, I want to thank my better half **Dr.Komal Aalyani** for inspiring and supporting me throughout the journey of writing this book. At the beginning, I was confused that how I will draft but she supported me a lot in drafting. I have written this just to inspire audience so that they can also make money online.

Coming with an idea and presenting it in your words is somehow difficult I can say. But on the other side it is also rewarding and interesting because you share some best ideas so people can learn from it.

If you are reading this book it means you are one of the dedicated leaders of your community.

Prologue

If you search on the Internet you will get many ways to make money online but in this book, you will get the best and outstanding ways you can try today to make money online. If you are hard-working and you have are passionate about making money online, you can definitely do it. NEVER SAY NO, JUST SAY YES I CAN MAKE MONEY ONLINE AND I CAN EARN WELL. Whether you are a student, working professional or a busy mother and you want to earn some extra penny- doing some interesting work online, your efforts can help you to make money from your home.

Sometimes we struggle in finding what would be best for us to make money online, and we think, will this particular way give us extra money? If this type of question has been running in your mind, you don't have to worry; you will get all the best ways here to make money online with your creative mind and your efforts.

Beware there are many money-making "scams" available on the internet, they will charge you Upfront fees and they will force you to work for them so STAY ALERT!

No matter in what skills you have the expertise or how much time available to you, you should get the best work, on this list you can start from today to make some extra money. After the years of research, I came up with the 21 genuine ways to make money online.

In some ways, you can just earn a few bucks in a month but other ways can be powerful money makers that fully depend on your time and how you are willing to invest your time into the given ways.

Read out all the best and exciting ways to make money online. You will get some of the ways that you have never heard before.

THE ART OF BLOGGING

BLOGGING sounds interesting, right? Those who have not heard anything about Blogging must give attention to this because from this you can earn millions of dollars. Its true many successful bloggers are already earning millions of dollars online, so why can't you? Blogging is the best way because you can do it anywhere. You just need a laptop, PC, and your creative mind. Yes, you will not get quick results, and not an easy way to make money, but if you have a passion for writing there are a lot of ways to make money with your writing skills.

Efforts, time, quality content, and a creative mind are the main ingredients if you want to get high success in Blogging. You can start Affiliate Marketing and promote other people's products through your writing skills, sell your own product, sell advertising on our blog, and many other ways available for you to start with. To build an audience will take time to make a decent amount of money, but yes once you build your high audience you can earn more than $10,000 per month. Blogging can generate passive income for you.

It requires very little time to set up a blog and Word Press CMS is the best you can go for it. You can create your blog within 15 minutes, you will get everything with Word Press ready-made templates, plugging, and much more you just have to setup as per your requirement. And yes you need hosting so I will recommend you to go with Blue Host Hosting, it is very best for you and officially recommended by Word Press itself, and the price of hosting is less than a cup of coffee! $2.95 a month.

You can start your journey in blogging with the Top Niches like:
Cooking
Health and fitness

Travel
Technology
Finance
and many others in which you have an interest.

Blogging is fun and you will connect with many people online who share similar interests just like you. Blogging is like you are running your own business because when you are making money from your blog you become a entrepreneur.

Publishing content to a blog is a way to independence from financial freedom. Like some other work, it will require some time and effort. Anyway being a blogger, you're steering the ship. You're the boss. You can work as per your time and schedule.

TWO
THE ART OF TAKING ONLINE SURVEYS

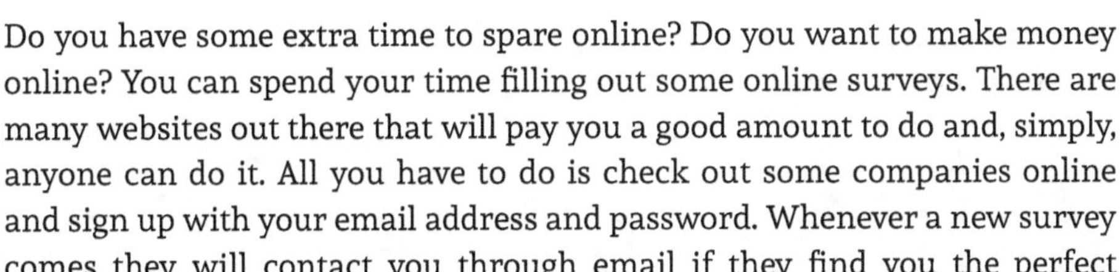

Do you have some extra time to spare online? Do you want to make money online? You can spend your time filling out some online surveys. There are many websites out there that will pay you a good amount to do and, simply, anyone can do it. All you have to do is check out some companies online and sign up with your email address and password. Whenever a new survey comes they will contact you through email if they find you the perfect match. So basically these surveys are for big brands and generally, they do online market research.

What can be simpler than responding to certain inquiries, communicating, and imparting your insights on surveys? Aside from being a simple assignment, paid surveys likewise take brief minutes to have the option to finish one survey and make money from it. So you just make sure that you have a reliable internet connection.

A very simple process to make money by answering online surveys or you can test the company products to make money from home. Ohh gosh you can also earn an extra $250 a month while watching TV it seems interesting and you must give it a try for this. In fact, online surveys are the best way to make some extra bucks online and you will make money with less effort.

Numerous people searching for approaches to make money online during their available time are confused about where to begin. They at times keep thinking about whether it will expect them to set up their website, sell products on the internet, and compose websites and write blogs, and much more to do. Notwithstanding your opinion, don't be debilitated for making money online is simpler than your opinion.

Their online surveys expect to help set up brands and organizations increase better

understanding of their expansive audience by methods for making consumers' voices heard. Honest feelings coming from honest people like you can surely help improve products and services, acquire critical change in the products being provided, and make a ground-breaking impact on future patterns.

Take a look at some paid survey websites below. The websites that I have mentioned you will make some extra money and also you will get gift vouchers too. You can signup for free and make money online from today.

Swagbucks
Survey Junkie
Inbox Dollars
OneOpinion
Pinecone Research

Alert: If a survey website asks you to pay money, be aware they might be a Scam.

THREE

THE ART OF BECOMING A FREELANCER OR FREELANCE WRITER

Well, you can earn thousands of dollars by getting freelancing work. Freelancing can definitely give rise to your income. You are at home and you have an English Degree in your hand, can you find mistakes in written text?

Many companies are hiring freelancers on a daily basis to do their task like content writing, proofreading, and much more and there is a lot of freelance work available online. There are many trusted websites out there but one which I want to recommend here is Upwork, when I talk about Upwork there are many employers there and they are constantly looking for freelancers and they are looking for people online to do all kind of tasks on their behalf.

If you want to start as a writer then you can write a business article or anything about technology and get paid for every single article you deliver to the client. So once you start growing, you can turn this into a full-time job.

Freelance writing is turning into a well-known professional decision for those who are looking for work from home. For a few, the opportunities related to career in freelance writing could exceed the real pay. For other people, freelance writing is an approach to sling themselves from the everyday routine of the all-day 9 to 5 Job.

You can also be a Ghost Writer, now you are confused about Ghost Writer right? So don't worry I will make it simple for you about it. It means Ghost Writer are those people who write Speeches, Journalistic works and some kind of other texts for other person who hire them.

At the point when you center around freelance writing as your essential type of income, you can definitely work from anyplace in the world. Some expert writers have accepted this as an open door to utilize freelance writing as a technique to subsidize their experiences. Others utilize freelance writing as an approach to remain at home and spend more time with their friends and families.

Along with freelance writing, you can also switch your mind on something like proofreading or transcription work. Many successful bloggers and authors are actively looking for proofreaders to make sure their writing is perfect or to the point.

FOUR

THE ART OF WORKING AS VIRTUAL ASSISTANT

Do you have a passion to enter the blogging field? Do you love writing and also posting on social media, but not looking forward to start your journey? I have a solution you can search for virtual assistant jobs where you can assist many people with their work. You can help other people to handle their website stuff and all the social media accounts. If you have the passion you can make this gig full time and make a high income online.

Well becoming a virtual assistant is an interesting option for those who want to work from home. Some people might be unaware of it but once you become a virtual assistant you will get many outstanding opportunities that are rapidly increasing with this remote computing technology.

When I talk about how much you can earn as a virtual assistant is unlimited you can earn high and unlimited. The very first thing when comes to mind is that you will get only certain hours of work and for the rate that you agreed with your client. Well, the fact is you will get more and more employment offers that you can handle.

At the starting point, you may need to set up your portfolio and get some positive reviews to build up your business from the clients that are willing to spend some amounts on your services that you agreed on. I studied that the most successful USA based virtual assistants charge higher to $50 to $100 per hour. If you are an expert in the particular Niche you could charge up to $20-$40 per hour. As you can see that there is a wide opportunity with great earnings. And when I talk about rates in the other country, the hourly rates are matching with the local rates.

The best successful virtual assistant business will subcontract work out to confide in entities and make measures that guarantee quality control. Right now the matter of virtual assistant is yet in the incipient stage, so the scope for your being in India is more.

FIVE

THE ART OF TEACHING ENGLISH ONLINE

Do you have a passion for teaching? Are you working as a teacher? Do you have at least one degree from college or university? If yes, then it is very good for you because you can teach English to children anywhere in the world.

Well, when you search on the Internet you will get many innovative online platforms that connect the English Teachers that have a degree to the other countries. You don't have to worry about it. Just sign up with the most popular platform when you search online, set a convenient time for class, and people from different countries will register for your class online. You can earn good money when you teach.

You can use this for a side hustle or you can make it a full-time career that totally depends on you. There are many good companies available, with them you can work more or as little as you like.

The Salaries of English Teachers depends on different factors:

The company you are working for.

The time you spend.

Degree and experience

Your base pay.

Many online English Teaching companies offer a flat rate of pay per hour or fixed price, well in other companies you can easily set your own hourly rate.

Frankly speaking, as per my research English Teachers are making anywhere between $10-50 USD per hour, but yes the rate fully depends on their degree and knowledge. If you are joining this for the first time and you have TEFL (Teaching English As A Foreign Language) certification. you will be making $10-$20 per hour at the starting point.

So the interesting thing is you can easily make money online and you can easily work from your home.

SIX

THE ART OF WRITING eBOOK

Do you have an interesting story and you want to share with everyone? Maybe you should make a plan to write an eBook and sell them on Amazon.

I have seen many authors, selling a ton eBooks on Amazon every year.

The online network has changed so many things in the world. EBooks and

Audio books are impressive ways to enlighten and create an experience for your followers. With e-books, you have opportunities to provide in-depth knowledge and guidance to your customers. You can pitch into the topic you have only delivered on your blogs or podcasts and create idle income in the process.

If you don't want to go for the blogging part, you can take the route of selling your eBook online and make money from it.

As internet entrepreneurs, we use mail and other social media sites to market our products and services and zoom to conduct meetings. And that's just small destruction on the internet. One of the biggest mixes up industries provides a great path to authoritative money-making online ventures for an entrepreneur in publishing and selling e-books online.

Amazing steps to create and sell ebooks e-books on your

Website:-

Do Research before selecting your book topic

Research the most searched keywords

Design your ebook

Format your ebook

Hire a graphic designer to design the layout and your

Ebook cover
Convert your eBook into other format
Add your eBook to the website
Advertise your eBook
While planning to list digital products keep in mind to research titles, sub-title, keywords, and pricing strategies for your eBook and blog content.

SEVEN

THE ART OF SELLING GIGS ON FIVERR

Fiverr is one of the most popular platforms to create online income and you can also provide your services called 'gigs' which help you in making money online. This is a place where freelancers make money online by offering their services to customers on a global scale.

With Fiverr, you can travel anywhere you want while putting skills to use and get paid. It is a place where you utilize your skill in a different manner.

If you don't know how you can start, I will say that you can check out the website a little bit and you will learn two things here:

You can see there are many different kinds of Gigs

Most of the freelancers charge more than $5- as $5 is just the baseline price.

What are Fiverr gigs?

It is a task provided by the seller. It can be anything logo design, software developer, content writer, etc.

How to make a gig:-

Step 1-Click on sales viewed on the top bar

Step 2-Click on create a brand new gig

Some type of gigs you can create :

Manage your social media gig

Content writing

Animation

Write comments on the blog

Narrate your video

Translation of language

Proofreading

A pop-up with creative business names

Influencer marketing

The most important part of Fiverr is the Gigs are set up in the way that allow clients to purchase your Gigs without even talking to you. It means if your Gigs are the perfect match for their requirements, you can make sales while you are sleeping at a time.

Write your Gig Description in a way that drives the mind of the buyer to purchase your Gig. You can convince the buyer in writing that you are the best person to do the task and you can make sure that you have all the experience that is required to complete the task.

The more you remain predictable on Fiverr, the more new opportunties that will open up for you. When you understand the framework, it will be simpler to explore and you'll have a superior understanding of how to make money on Fiverr.

EIGHT

THE ART OF SELLING STOCK PHOTOS

Get ready to know about how you can make money by selling stock photos.

Stock photography is one of the most powerful ways to make passive income. You can make money just by uploading your photos for others and you can put a price for your photos so if someone likes it then they can purchase and you will get paid. It is a very simple and easy method of making money just by taking photos and you can do it from your home with less effort. So as a photographer simply just submit your photos on stock photography websites and earn money each time when someone purchases your photos.

Stock photography websites may not give you a high source of income as per your expectation but the money that you will earn is simply worth it. For the first time, you have to sign up as a content provider on the website after that you have to submit the images for approval. Once your image is approved then you can make money easily.

When you are going to start selling, **JUST THINK BIG PICTURE IN MIND.** Don't expect high returns in the initial months. Work continuously and put a high contribution to the website and you will see a high difference in your earnings.

How much money can you make? A big question?

It completely depends on the number of images you have added to your portfolio.

How well you have put your keywords into your images.

How you are going to fulfill the demands of your customers.

At last, it depends on how you are passionate about stock photography.

Three Important Tips just keep in mind:

Keywords For Images

Continuously Keep the End-user in Mind

Upload photos on a daily basis.

If you have a passion for photography and really want some extra bucks through your photography skills, then stock photography is the best and perfect way to earn some extra income online.

Take some unique photos that people love, research, upload regularly and I just say you should definitely earn up to $500/month.

What are you waiting for? Do you want to give a quick start?

NINE
THE ART OF CREATING ONLINE COURSES

Do you have skills and that you want to teach and share? You can teach on any topic that you have expertise in at sites like Udemy. There are many courses out there about anything and many people are making money online just by creating courses. You can create a course which you find the perfect and you can put the pricing as per your knowledge that is perfect for you.

Sharing your best knowledge with the world is one of the most creative ways to make money online. If you are an expert in any subject, you can share your knowledge just by creating online courses. Create a course for your audiences and sell it on Udemy, also if you have a great audience on your website or on social media you can also sell there too. I have seen some entrepreneurs earning very high about $5000 per month just by creating online courses and selling. You can also try this and set your passive income.

Search what other people are doing, you can check other courses that are related to your topic and try to do something unique for your course if you want to be successful. You can also check their reviews of what people like the most so you can plan your online course accordingly. How can you create something unique from others? Focus more on your content and try to solve the problems also so that people will learn something new from your course.

If you are selling your course on Udemy, you don't have to worry about the promotion. You just upload your course and sit back and relax. If you plan to host your course on your own website you can run ads to promote it. You can also build an email list to promote the courses.

In this Internet era people are searching for many things including entertainment
and socializing and the internet is very useful to find and learn some creative things.

Many people are creating blogs or they plan to write books, but the online course is also another method to set your passive income.

Quick steps to create an online course today:

Select course topic

Market Research

Outline your course

Search for the best methods to deliver your course in front of your audience.

Create your lessons

Upload your course

Market your course

Make Money from your course

Once your course is uploaded online you can simply make passive income from it.

TEN

THE ART OF AMAZON MECHANICAL TURK

As in this world most of the people look for the source where they can make money from home. Some are looking for full-time opportunities, and others are very happy by spending their time to earn extra money. Maybe people would be happy by earning upto $10 a day online with some small tasks, that depends on your condition and how much time you can spare.

There are many people in the world making money online everyday with their own comfort and own timings and whenever they want from the most trusted platform called Amazon Mechanical Turk (MTurk). This is the most legitimated marketplace run by Amazon. You will get some short tasks that are suitable for the people those who are looking to work from home.

As the pay is low, you can set it as the primary source of income as many people are drawn to MTurk. But it could be the best way for those who are looking to earn some extra bucks in their spare time. You can do the task while watching TV commercial breaks or during your lunch hour so there is no time limit and you can complete the task anytime.

When I talk about MTurk is a flexible remote and online working opportunity for anyone who has completed 18 years and has a stable internet connection.

Simply realize that there's a trial period where you may not meet all requirements for more lucrative HITs — be patient! As a result of its adaptability. Most other remote positions require a set timetable that may not be helpful for stay-at-home guardians, undergraduates, occupied retired folks and people in the middle of occupations.

Pick micro from Amazon Mechanical Turk. These are services that require human cooperation. You can telecommute, adaptable hours and get paid by one of the world's biggest retailers.

Below are the list of example task that people have completed already:

Compare the two products

Check out the item number for the product picture.

Select the right spelling from the words given.

Check about this website is best for the audience?

Select the right category for the particular product.

Translate a paragraph from one language to another.

The price mentioned for each task may vary, and it depends on the person who has posted the task and the HIT. Various requesters pay various rates, so the sum you can acquire for finishing the task that is endorsed by the requester can change enormously. You can acquire as meager as 1 penny for the task that is endorsed by the requester.

If you can work rapidly on assignments that premium you to finish, you can get more cash-flow at all measures of time. You may discover HITs that pay $0.15 each however just take around 15 seconds to finish. If you could finish whatever number of these HITs as would be prudent, your profit could include rapidly over the long haul.

If you give your proper time then yes it is possible that you can earn $100 a week. Most of the people in the world are making more than $500 per month on the Amazon Turk Site.

Amazon Turk is an extraordinary work from home opportunity for the people if you need to make additional money in your extra time. If you are in any event 18-year-old, you can join here as a Worker on the Amazon MTurk website to start making money online from today.

ELEVEN

THE ART OF BOOKKEEPING

If you are searching for a new position or even only a side hustle, this might be something that you need to investigate. Figuring out how to turn into a virtual bookkeeper can be an extraordinary career choice. You don't need to be an accountant or have any past

involvement with requests to begin freelance bookkeeping!

Bookkeeping is also the best way to make money online.

Customary bookkeepers are very common, yet incredible bookkeepers – who genuinely have the entrepreneur's wellbeing on the most fundamental level – were so tricky.

Each business is required (and should) track each dollar that comes into their business or goes out. In principle, this appears to be pretty simple. Practically speaking, it simply isn't so.

The bookkeeper is the entrepreneur who depends on exact monetary data. Entrepreneurs want to be able to spotlight the skills that they are very good at and delegate the tasks that they are not very great at. When I talk about Bookkeeping, it is one of the perfect examples of a task that smart entrepreneurs outsource their work to others.

Common customers are little to medium-sized entrepreneurs who are in need of somebody who can HELP them; somebody who knows a great deal is attractive and has their back with regards to bookkeeping.

This is one of the most well-known questions. It truly is 100% ward upon how much effort, time, and care one places into the beginning and developing their own virtual bookkeeping business.

The capacity to work remotely (or anyplace you pick) is extraordinary. You will decide when you work, where you work, and with whom you work.

You don't have to have any past involvement in bookkeeping or accounting. That is another positive part of turning into a bookkeeper. Truly, that implies that you can figure out how to turn into a bookkeeper with no experience.

Along these lines, the magnificence of having your own virtual bookkeeping business is that you can utilize a worth estimating model where you have a set monthly fee instead of an hourly rate. When your customer concedes to a rate then you will utilize all the highlights of the online products to make your employment constantly easy and simple.

Make $40,000 every Year From Home as a Bookkeeper – If you need to earn money from home and love numbers and aiding entrepreneurs, at that point this is a side hustle that will work for you!

Important Tip:

Get your work done BEFORE you make a go at a bookkeeping business. Make certain it's a business worth your time and monetary investment.

After you've done your due diligence, focus on being a success. Leave yourself no other alternative except to be a hit with your business.

TWELVE

THE ART OF ONLINE COACHING AND CONSULTING.

Coaching and consulting are one of the main ways that you should start with and it is regularly perhaps the most straightforward approach to make money online if you have a good audience and visitors. At the point when you're a specialist or expertise in your market, individuals will frequently search you out for help and guidance.

There's potential for coaching and consulting in practically any industry – regardless of whether it be health, fitness, dating, business, money, investing, online marketing, and many more.

Whether you're now guiding customers or simply considering to get started for this, taking your service online can help discover a larger number of customers and get more money than you expected.

Coaching and counseling require time. You can consider it as a "passive income source" by any measure and doing it implies you're actually stuck in the worldview of exchanging your time for money. However long you're exchanging your time for money, you'll always be unable to scale up your pay or have the opportunity.

The most concerning issue with online coaching and business counseling is that it requires some time than alternate ways we've covered to make money online.

You'll have to regularly be finding new customers, addressing their requirements and afterward getting more customers... it's a hamster wheel!

Online Coaching is certainly not an easy revenue source, yet not many of the approaches to bring in huge money are detached.

The secret to getting more money consulting is to robotize how much of your process could be expected. This implies computerizing both your business cycle and consulting.

Payscale records the middle time-based compensation for Life Coaches at $30.42 every hour except the reach differs from $11.37 to $103.50 every hour and yearly pay rates go as high as $200,000+ every year. The middle compensation would work out to simply over $60,000 per year if you were working an all-day gig.

You will be your own boss with your own company and that implies...

You can get as much money as you need!

You're not simply making money for your time, you're procuring what it's worth to transform someone's life!

Rather than evaluating your consulting continuously, charge as indicated by results. Mention to individuals what issues you will tackle and what needs you will help them satisfy. A ton of times, those requirements are priceless so you can charge decent amount.

In the wake of working with a couple of customers, you'll improve your feel for what amount of time and work it requires to fulfill your promises. You'll have the option to change your costs higher or lower to locate that fair compromise among worth and getting more money.

There are a couple of things you can do to make your online consulting business to get high success.

Zero in on specialty inside a solitary thought. It will help you master the theme and stand out among the wide range of various coaches.

Your coaching should take care of an issue. Individuals would prefer not to 'find out' about your extraordinary new procedure, they need to take care of their concern to which it relates.

Making money consulting or as an online mentor might be one of the principal ways you consider to make income from your blog or it might require a long time to develop it. It's one of the more lucrative online pay sources however sets aside an effort to build the prospect and experience to be effective. Whichever way you choose to take, don't tally out the estimation of your experience, and don't neglect this powerful method to make money online.

THIRTEEN

THE ART OF AFFILIATE MARKETING

Do you want to put your step into Affiliate Marketing and make money online, but you are a bit confused about how you can start?

Affiliate Marketing is about earning lots of money just by sitting and without giving any effort ? This is what a quick Google search would have you believe, but the truth is somehow different than that.

Yes, You can make money with your full efforts with Affiliate Marketing. A great amount of money and another thing is you can make money while you sleep this is the power of Affiliate Marketing.

If you have a high online presence in social media or you have good visitors on your blog or website you can start earning high money immediately just by promoting the companies products, services, and offers online.

One best thing is that it is one of the cheapest and easiest ways to do marketing online. You don't have to create and sell a product. Only one thing you have to do is to create a connection between buyer and seller and take your commission then they buy something from the affiliate link. That's how affiliate marketing works.

Once you join the Affiliate program, you will get the unique Affiliate link and you can promote the link on social media platforms and just create the connection and earn a commission. Sounds pretty interesting right?

Many big brands offer an affiliate program. We can take an example of Amazon here: the affiliate program run by Amazon is Amazon Associates. The affiliate program is of any industry like health and fitness, travel, real estate, etc. You can sign up for the program which one you select and get your unique tracking link and you can use this link to promote products. You can also write the product review and put that link in that review.

Affiliate marketing is the passive earning source but on the other hand, it is highly competitive but still, I can say that you can make millions of dollars online with Affiliate Marketing.

Just check some basics of how Affiliate Marketing Works:

Promote product or services to your audiences through your website, blog, or social media

Your audience purchase the product using your affiliate link

You will earn a commission if someone purchases the product from your link.

Useful tips you must consider if you want to start affiliate marketing:

Be Patient

Go with more attractive products

Use various traffic channels

Test and measure performance

Research the demand for the product

Try unique methods and tricks

Use tools

Attract targeted traffic

There are the quick steps you should consider to make money online with Affiliate Marketing. Affiliate marketing is a great source of income and you can make money from home. Just create a blog or website, write unique articles, attract visitors to your website, and join some best affiliate programs. In writing, it seems that it is very easy, but yes you should be patient until you reach your goal and make sales. Work and work, put your efforts, start earning money from home, and make money as an affiliate.

FOURTEEN

THE ART OF CREATING VIDEOS

Do you watch YouTube Videos daily? Obviously, do! This is one of the world's most mainstream sites, with over 2 billion users watching a huge number of long hours of video each day.

You can use YouTube's reach to make money online. No, you're doing whatever it takes not to make a viral video, in a manner of speaking, in fact, if it goes worldwide and is seen by millions, that is something worth being thankful for.

All things considered, you'll be after a proven strategy to increase views on different videos consistently. You'll be making helpful content—something engaging that individuals need to watch. Also, it works in many, various niches. It very well may be a how-to video or a talking-head video on a subject of interest for individuals in your niche—anything is possible.

You make money with advertisement income. Your initial step is to make a YouTube account and begin uploading videos. At that point, you empower monetization on your YouTube settings. Basically, this gives Google the thumbs up to incorporate short AdSense ads with your videos, which you've checked whether you've viewed a YouTube video. At the point when viewers click on those promotions, you get paid.

Another way to make money with a YouTube channel is through paid sponsorships. Make high viewers on your YouTube channel and the big companies will gladly pay you to promote or make reference to their products and services in your videos

A few tips to make professional-looking videos.

The most important thing is that you can also use your smartphone to upload your videos or you make use of the simple video camera both are good to go. In any case, ensure the lighting is good so everything in your video is clear and simple to see.

Make sure the sound is understood. You don't need a cooling hum, development noise, or different interruptions.

There are many good video editing software available you can simply put the title at the beginning of the video and to edit anything you want.

Most importantly, recall that your videos can be straightforward and don't need to be smooth. Simply give valuable content and be connected with and interesting. Entertaining helps as well.

What's more, to expand the reach for your videos, make sure to post them on your Facebook business page, Twitter, your blog, and different channels. You can simply tell your audience that you're in the video business now.

Notwithstanding advertisement income from YouTube videos, you can likewise utilize your YouTube channel to drive traffic back to your site, where your audience can check your products that you are selling, click on the advertisements on your site, or even get onto your email list—where you can make different deals with your email list.

FIFTEEN

THE ART OF TESTING WEBSITES AND APPS

Are you looking for some best and extraordinary ways to make money to test websites and apps online?

This seems like a very entertaining and interesting way to make money online.

If it is like that you can scroll down and check out how you can make money to test websites and mobile apps.

Why test websites and mobile apps? Actually, the main focus is to improve the presence of the website online so that users can check the website without any difficulty. To do this many companies hire just real people like you to test the new or existing websites and apps. So that the website and app owner can see the results of the obstacles that they have on the website so that they can improve quickly.

If you want to get started, you will need to be an internet expert and have a good command of the English Language. Along with that, you need some basic tools like a computer with a microphone, camera, and stable internet connection, and a well-updated browser. Generally, most of the tests take an average time of 5-25 minutes to finish, and pay on average is $10 per test.

Below are some of the companies mentioned to visit if you want to make money to test websites and apps online:

1. User Testing
2. Test Birds
3. TrymyUI
4. Userzoom
5. Ferpection

Presently, in case you're in any way similar to me, you're multiplying the number of tests you can finish in an hour and the amount you will make. Yet, wait for a minute or two! These open doors are very popular! There are fewer clients than testers, so don't anticipate finishing three tests each hour at the top of the hour.

Below are some of the best way you can follow to increase your chance of making extra money:

1. Don't stick to one website, signup for as many as you can- so the more sites you will register you will get a high opportunity to make a high income.
2. Be certain that you're exploiting practice and sample t testing openings, the same number of companies will just let you two or multiple times to pass through their test.
3. Continuously make a point to turn in your most ideal work, the same number of companies rate their testers, and those with higher scores will in general improve paying gigs.

Have a good rating – Most websites on this rundown have reviews and ratings for every one of their testers. If your rating is high, you'll land more positions. Ensure that you are giving quality input and after the tester rules on each site.

The way that you can get paid to test sites and applications from home with no related knowledge is really great. In case you're a beginner hoping to begin testing sites, I enthusiastically suggest evaluating user testing.

While you're not going to get rich doing site testing, it is a simple and adaptable approach to acquire some extra money. If such a work is engaging, likewise take a stab at looking at Web Search Evaluating positions — this post will show to you about it.

SIXTEEN

THE ART TO BECOME MASTER IN PODCASTING

Well this method is for the people who are comfortable to speak in front of a microphone, so are you the one? Do you want to start podcasting with just a microphone?

What amount would you be able to earn once you start podcasting: the business standard for podcast sponsorships begins at $15-$18 per 800-1000 listens in for pre-move sponsorships (toward the start of the podcast), $25 for mid-move (some place in the digital podcast scene) and $10 for post-move (toward the finish of your podcast) – so your profit will rely upon how attractive your podcast gets. Or however, another approach to make money from podcasting is to start affiliate marketing and promote the affiliate products.

While you can possibly begin doing it for free, and yes on the other hand if you are very serious about podcasting it merits getting some tool to guarantee the sound is adequate; fortunately, since podcasting is so trendy now, there are a lot of podcasting units that you can get that join all you must (microphone, earphones, and so on) and can cost somewhere in the range of $100 to $1,000 (yet you can take care of business with less expensive packs!)

If you passion for presenting some knowledge with your talks – particularly with others as well – podcasting can be an incredible method to make money online.

As you've seen before, you can definitely start to make money from podcasting when you have a decent base of audience members for every one of your episodes, so it will take some effort to get your podcast to that level so you can make money from it. However, when you do get to a specific level, you can really make in tons of money from podcasting

Along these lines, the potential is certainly there – and podcasting is at a point where it's actually growing in fame across the world, not yet immersed.

Yet, much the same as with publishing blog content earlier, you need to pick a best niche, one with a ton of potential. Also, if you need your podcast to expand and get more audience members with each scene, at that point you need to put your much time in promoting your podcast on various platforms.

Some tips to select a best niche to get started with Podcasting:

Prepare a list of your skills and what you can do.

Do some research about your competition

Select the format of your podcast

Think about your future.

SEVENTEEN

THE ART OF CREATING E-COMMERCE STORE AND SELL YOUR PRODUCTS

It's for anyone who want to build their online business and make money. If you have products to sell you can create an e-commerce store and sell your products online and make money.

You could be making barely enough to keep above each month or you could go to **Asos**- And check their success and how they are growing. Everything relies upon your products, the service you can give, the productivity of your niche and your marketing methods – making a great product isn't enough to get high success. There are a variety of components that make up an effective ecommerce business however if you get every one of them right, at that point the potential outcomes are very high.

It can cost you a bit to begin an online business; you'll need to get hosting and an ecommerce tool to make your site; you'll need to think about assembling costs ; material costs and shipping costs. There are many things you have to consider before jump into the ecommerce business.

There are 2 main points you have to consider for e-commerce business:

Either make and sell your own products, which you've planned and made (obviously, not in a real sense – you can pay others to produce your plan for you)

Or however sell products made by others, which you buy at discount cost and afterward sell them at a greater cost

The primary alternative has the greater potential for productivity; that is because when you sell another person's products you can indeed check them up a limited amount of a lot so you're just making a little level of benefit with every deal.

With products you make yourself, then again, you can price them whatever amount of you need, and as a rule, the benefit will be greater too.

Nonetheless, it's additionally much more work; you'll need to:

Design your products.

Search for a good producer that can transform your plans into a reality and that can convey as guaranteed.

Find and buy quality materials for your item at a reasonable cost

Set up a good transportation system as else, you'll be eaten up right away by conveyance giants like Amazon

What's more, these are only a portion of the perspectives that you'll have to consider if you will make and sell your own items.

Yet, as I stated, the advantage is that your benefits will be higher as well.

Furthermore, the other choice isn't without its dangers possibly; you'll need to buy enough stock to have available so that can be an enormous investment on your part that probably won't pay off.

Also, the benefits, as I clarified earlier, will be lower too.

That being stated, it's substantially less of an issue than having to really make the products and manage the manufacturing side of things, so it's a lot simpler to begin with this method.

EIGHTEEN

THE ART OF DROP-SHIPPING

So once again I will tell you that it is also one of the easiest ways to make money online. Let's check out how you can make money with Dropshipping.

Do you want to start an e-commerce business and you don't want to take all the headache of manufacturing, shipping ? Then is the best way for you to get started. YES, THIS IS FOR YOU.

What amount would you be able to earn: not so much; the overall revenue is a lot lower since the maker or distributor you'll work with will handle all the significant costs (manufacturing, storing, transporting, and so forth)

Start-up expenses: while the overall revenue is a lot lower than with other e-commerce websites, so are the beginning up expenses: since you don't have to buy or store any products, all you truly must is website hosting and a perfect theme to start with and plugin to assemble and deal with your online store – all in all, your costs will be lower than $100 every month

Dropshipping is like a fast beginning way to begin an online business: you don't need to make or even buy any products, you don't need to store them and you don't need to ship them once somebody puts an order.

All in all, what is Dropshipping?

It's a type of trade where you join partner with a product manufacturer (or a distributor) to sell their products – essentially, you work the store and work to get new clients and promote the products, while they handle the rest:

Planning the product

Manufacturing the entire product.

A place to store the product.

Shipping the products, when somebody orders it.

It's a much simpler approach to begin to make money online and what's more, the dangers included are impressively lower.

However, as I referenced earlier, that likewise implies that your profit will be a lot lower as well.

When beginning an online business, one of the key components is having products to sell. So how would you get products, where do you discover them, how would you know whether they'll sell, and how would you get them to customers?

There is an answer that permits you to avoid every one of those problems. Also, it makes the entire startup measure for your online business a lot simpler. It's called dropshipping. Also, it has overwhelmed the online business world. A drop shopping business is one of the quickest, least demanding, and low risky approaches to start with an online business.

Dropshipping is one of the easiest ways to make money with less effort.

An online dropshipping business is a snappy, simple, and generally, safe approach to begin selling on the internet. You won't need to give a lot of money forthright on a stock that probably won't sell, your drop shipping partner will deal with all conveyances to your clients.

Pick the correct niche market and item, and you could have a beneficial venture on your hands. You could even venture into different niches and sell different products, as well.

NINETEEN

THE ART OF EMAIL MARKETING

Well, this method is for anyone who can put their efforts to make money online. If you have a good email list, I am sure you can make high earnings with Email Marketing. But one thing is very important to understand, it takes time to make a decent email list and start making money. But yes once you start with a proper strategy then no one can stop you from making money online and you will keep growing.

To get started you need an Email Marketing Tool. Well once you search on the Internet you will get many tools but here I will suggest you to go with ConvertKit to send the automated tools to your email list that you have built. You also need a Landing page. You can try some landing page builder online to host your subscription form.

You can earn millions of dollars with Email Marketing- If you have a good idea, you can kickstart and convert many clients.

Here's how it works:

You make a landing page for a one-page site where the audience can join your list and you clarify why they should join.

You set up an opt-in form to begin gathering names and email addresses for your email list – as I referenced earlier, Here I will suggest you try OptinMonster.

Get an email marketing tool like ConvertKit to begin sending emails to your email list, including automated emails and automated email successions.

You can also register with a relevant affiliate program, after that you can promote affiliate links and services with the proper content to your email list. Once people will sign up you can make money. This is a profoundly powerful approach to make money with an email list and the more your list grows, the more your income will generate. With the correct method and a big email list, you can stand making even a huge amount dollars a month.

Send ordinary email broadcasts to your email marketing list, utilizing ConvertKit; some do this every day, some week after week – it's up to you how often you need to send an email. In any case, it's essential to make sure that you set a schedule and stick to it – and illuminate your list too about how often you will email them, precisely.

Below are the topics you can cover in your email:

You can send daily marketing tips

You can send some cooking recipes

You can send a motivational email

You can send some health and fitness tips

As you grow day by day and if you have a high subscriber, you can even make your own products and you can sell them via email- this is also a great way to make money with email marketing.

Examples of own products you can make:

Ebooks

Templates

Online Courses

Membership sites.

If you are very serious about making money online you must try the Email Marketing Method.

TWENTY

THE ART OF CREATING AND SELLING WEBINARS

This is for the people who have other products or services to sell or promote or ability that they can instruct others.

The money you make with the webinar is between like hundred or thousand dollars for each online webinar

It requires a small amount of investment to get started and it is up to $50-$100 every month – all you must is a webinar software, however the valuing as a rule relies upon the number of participants you have.

Webinars can be a creative way to make money online and it can be used in many ways.

You can use it and promote a product or service that you want to offer to other people so that they can buy and you make money. You can create a free webinar.

Yes, you can also make money just by promoting affiliate products and make money from the affiliate sales you get.

Sell webinars straightforwardly by offering enough worth.

Every choice can be highly adequate and can help you to earn serious money if you select some good topic and have an outstanding marketing strategy. Here are some of the best tips and tricks to recall about webinars.

There are a few unique sorts of webinars: like live webinars to solve the queries of the person (they occur at a specific time and are recorded live), on-demand webinar s(pre-recorded online classes that people can watch at any second), automated webinars (online classes that occur at a specific time yet are recorded already)

Webinars commonly run for 45 minutes + 15 extra minutes toward the finish of the webinars, saved for a Q&A meeting

You'll have to make the best landing page for your webinar – this is the place where people will enlist; the best news is, you can make use of ClickMeeting to make and host your webinar with the best tool,; this is additionally the page you'll use to promote your webinar that you are going to start and should contain all the significant data with respect to the date and time, just as the thing participants will escape your webinar.

Make use of email marketing by sending automated emails so that people can register. From that people will get all the proper information about the webinar. Also if you want people to register try to send an email on regular basis to remind them about the webinar,

Prepare extra resources and materials that will be helpful for your seminar. Also, give away free materials to your attendees to give more value and attract them to buy.

TWENTY-ONE

THE ART OF PROOF-READING AND EDITING

This is a very interesting way for those to have a good command of English Grammar and for those who are enthusiastic readers.

When I tell you about earnings the chances are very high, like about $10-$30 per 1000 words on very well-known freelancing websites like Fiverr. So likewise if you can give full dedication this way you'd earn about $2000-$4500 for a book. Yes, it's true and sounds interesting also.

You can start for free, yes it is true no investment needed for this side hustle. Although it would be valuable to buy the premium plan of an important tool like grammar to help you to get more Grammar errors. It is a much more powerful tool than a regular tool and can carry out more errors.

If you have a passion for reading and you're Grammar mistakes this may very well be the ideal route for you to make some extra money online with less effort.

Also, in this time when in a real sense anybody with an Internet connection can independently publish effectively, there's a ton of work to go around.

Plus, it's not simply writers that need editing and proofreading services; bloggers, organizations, and such often make complex bits of content that must some extra attention to carry out the mistakes.

Besides, you don't need a bachelor's degree in English (or another language) to get started; as a specialist, you can move immediately – If you're not perfect at that point that will talk in of itself.

Proofreading is one of the best online jobs that should be possible from pretty much anyplace and you can start with any device.

If you are looking to start freelancing, you'll need to effectively showcase yourself. And if you want to start work for a brand or company, you'll generally be reacting to jobs posted on different online job posting websites. What's more, some of the time, you'll get freelance proofreading work looking through online.

However, it is much important to understand that solving mistakes in a book isn't simply proofreading; it's much more than that; you likewise should be extremely mindful of things like:

Character improvement

Plot irregularities

Language and style irregularities

Clarity and legitimacy

So it's not simply a straightforward instance of evolving "their" to "there" or shortening a couple of sentences to a great extent; rather, it's agreement on what the writer needs to get across, what their message is, and who are their characters so you can give productive comments that will truly help improve their writing.

Freelance proofreading work regularly gives flexibility. By and large, your committed work can be finished when of the day or night, as long as you fulfill your customer's timeline.

That implies you might have the option to proofread as a side-hustle inspite of your regular 9 to 5 job.

Not at all like with many work-at-home opportunities, you don't really must a personal computer to succeed. There are people making money by editing on different gadgets, such as, laptops or tablets. Mechanical advances have made it unbelievably simple to share files far and wide.

At last, added that proofreading work is very good for you to get started and make money online. There are a huge number of content creators around the world looking to hire people to polish their work.

You can take a training test to check whether you think proofreading is something you'd prefer to seek after further.

Roll Up

Since you've made it to the furthest limit of this in fact extremely long, epic guide on the most proficient method to make money online, it's quite clear that you needn't bother with a time machine to return to the 90's to make money online. There are, indeed, plenty of opportunities for basically any aptitude level, information and age – and even the degree of involvement from your part and the sum you need to make.

If you need to bring in some extra money each month, you have many alternatives to browse.

What's more, if you need to make a huge number of dollars consistently, you can: you'll simply have to attempt to do it.

www.ingramcontent.com/pod-product-compliance
Lightning Source LLC
Chambersburg PA
CBHW060916130726

48001CB00006B/2266